So You Wanna Be A Landlord

Millie

authorHOUSE®

AuthorHouse™
1663 Liberty Drive
Bloomington, IN 47403
www.authorhouse.com
Phone: 1-800-839-8640

First published by AuthorHouse   3/30/2010

ISBN: 978-1-4490-8881-1 (e)
ISBN: 978-1-4490-8880-4 (sc)

Printed in the United States of America
Bloomington, Indiana

This book is printed on acid-free paper.

DEDICATION

I would like to dedicate this book to my son, Garrie Mitchell and my two grandsons, Robert Mitchell and Gerald Mitchell.

My son worked for hours to get this into the proper format and on a tape.

My two grandsons started helping me when they were 12 yrs old. It started with cutting the grass at the duplexes, helping me lay carpet and clean up.

As they got older they painted walls, hung ceiling fans and replaced faucet washers.

They are grown men now with families of their own. Gerald is still close by and he is my right hand man when I need help.

There's nothing like family.

Contents

BOOK SUMMARY   IX

CHAPTER 1   A Soldier's Wife and Baby   1

CHAPTER 2   The Couple from Australia   6

CHAPTER 3   One child, fourteen cats and a dog   9

CHAPTER 4   A Mom Tries to Straighten Out Her Son   13

CHAPTER 5   A Father Reunites With His Son   18

CHAPTER 6   A Real Gentleman   20

CHAPTER 7   The Taxi Driver   23

CHAPTER 8   Aware Of Constant Maintenance   29

CHAPTER 9   Dead Tenant   32

CHAPTER 10   Girls From The Strip Tease Club   34

CHAPTER 11   A Sister And Two Brothers   38

CHAPTER 12   The Burned Out College Graduate   42

CHAPTER 13   The Perfect Tenant   45

CHAPTER 14   A mother and child   48

CHAPTER 15   A hard worker – A heavy drinker   51

CHAPTER 16   Jewelry Store Owners   54

CHAPTER 17   Good Old Jimmy   58

CHAPTER 18   What happened to Dan?   62

CHAPTER 19   A Friend wants In   65

CHAPTER 20   A Volunteer Painter   67

CHAPTER 21   Renting To Relatives   69

CHAPTER 22   A Sad Story For Mother And Son   71

CHAPTER 23   Too Many People For A Small Room   73

CHAPTER 24   The Odd Couple   75

CHAPTER 25   A Son On Drugs   77

CHAPTER 26	Three Vietnamese Refugees	79
CHAPTER 27	It's Later Than We Think	81
CHAPTER 28	Do Your Homework Before You Move	83
CHAPTER 29	Exchanged Furniture	85
CHAPTER 30	The Trespasser	87
CHAPTER 31	Who Owns The Vehicle?	92
CHAPTER 32	In Conclusion	95
AUTHOR'S BIOGRAPHY		97

Book Summary

I've entitled my book "So You Wanna be a Landlord" because through the years I've heard some of my friends say, "What a life, you just sit back and collect rent". Well, after you read about some of my experiences, you'll change your mind about "Just sitting back".

I've owned rental property for 40 years and I've only rented "Furnished Apartments" Maybe in my mind I'm forcing my tenants to live up to the standard of living I set. I'm a woman but I've laid many, many carpets with the help of my son and grandsons.

I've always furnished my apartments nice and I feel that I could live in any one of them myself. The living room always has a couch, two matching lounge chairs, two end tables, two lamps, and a coffee table. The bedrooms have a full or queen size bed, two changes of sheets and pillow- cases, a dresser, a nightstand table and 2 lamps. The bathroom has 6 hand towels, 3 bath towels and 3 washcloths. The kitchen has a table and 4 chairs, matching dishes, stainless steel tableware, stainless steel cookware and a frying pan.

When Broyhill Furniture Co. had a warehouse in our area they sold new and rental furniture. There are often real bargains to pick up and I bought returned rental furniture from them many times.

I always carry the room sizes with me when I need carpet. I visit the carpet warehouses so I'm ready to pick up a carpet remnant at a good price. The carpet is never fastened to a tacking strip, it is laid loose wall to wall with double stick carpet tape around the edges, and it works well.

Renting out furnished apartments has some advantages and some disadvantages. Sometimes tenants take

sheets, towels and pillowcases when they leave, but that's about it. I find that pillowcases are a favorite because all the small items can be thrown in the pillow- case, tied at the open end, and then thrown in the car. I furnish lawn service and I pay the electric for the entire building. The tenant gets a copy of the electric bill and pays it when the rent is paid.

It's a business, so I expect that everything is not going to be perfect. As you read about some of my experiences you'll understand what I mean. I don't argue with my tenants and I never socialize with them. friends and business don't mix. I'm friendly, but not as a pal or as a social friend. I check the garage sales because there are many bargains there too. Consignment shops are another place to get good bargains. Church sales are also good.

I don't try to get the highest rent in the area. I'm middle of the road, and most of my tenants are long term. If they have a problem I have it taken care of immediately. I have a plumber and electrician who I can call and get quick service. Most of the other jobs I have been able to do myself, sometimes with the help of my son or grandsons.

Living reasonably close to the property is a "must". I've seen some property destroyed because the Landlord lived "out of state" and the tenants knew it. I like to drive by my property every week, if possible.

Being a landlord takes a lot of patience and understanding, but rental property is a good investment and has provided additional income for many years.

CHAPTER 1

A Soldier's Wife and Baby

I used to think I was a fairly good judge of people, but I'm willing now to admit that you can't judge a book by it's cover. Just by meeting a prospective tenant is not enough time to form a realistic opinion of their character or behavior.

Take for example the nice young people who showed up to rent my three-bedroom house on the lake. One young lady was carrying a baby about 9 months old and she was the one interested in renting the house. She introduced the other young lady as her sister and the young man who was with them was supposedly their brother. She explained that her husband was in the service and had 6 months to go before he would be coming home She and her sister would live in the house and both work at a nearby restaurant where they would be working different shifts so one would always be home with the baby. She walked around the beautiful yard on the lake side and remarked that her husband would be so happy to come home to such a beautiful place, and when he got home they would start to plan their future.

It sure sounded good, and I was a sucker for seeing that the baby had a nice home. Well, the other young lady wasn't her sister and the young man wasn't her brother but I didn't know that until about 3 months later. Money was no problem so we sat down and went over the Rental Agreement that I used.

I was renting the house "furnished" because we had been using it as a summer home and at this time we felt we were not in a financial position to maintain the expense of two homes so we decided to rent one out.

Within a month I got several calls from the neighbors at the lake house. They said the girls had an unusually active social life. There were cars parked up and down the street – all visiting the two girls. I was concerned because I really didn't appreciate this much wear and tear on the furniture but the rent arrived on time (even a few days early). I didn't follow through on my hunch to drive out and see what was going on. At the end of the second month my lake neighbors were calling and reporting real wild stories. The police were there a couple times a week and the number of people going "in and out" was unbelievable. Things were just "not right". The rent arrived on time again and due to the fact that I had to drive 40 miles to the lake house, I kept putting it off.

Finally about the third week of the third month I got a call from my lake neighbor who said she was sure the girls had moved because they were seen carrying suitcases out to their car, including a lot of baby things I drove out to see what was going on.

They were right, the girls had moved, but the condition of the house was enough to make me sit down and cry. The front door was a "French Door". Two panes of glass were missing, one even with the doorknob and one even with the dead bolt above the doorknob. Anybody could gain access to the house by reaching in and turning the doorknob and the dead bolt. There were at least 40 empty wine bottles sitting around on the glassed in porch facing the lake. The toilet was not working. Apparently something had been thrown in which would not allow it to flush. As a result, several people had used the bathtub for a toilet and the odor was sickening. All the light bulbs were missing. There were cigarette burns on the tabletops and furniture. There were wine stains on all the carpets and the stove looked like it had never been cleaned while they were there. On the stove was a pan of half cooked beans and a frying pan with several burnt pork chops.

Most surprising of all was that each closet in each bedroom had a peep hole about 3" in diameter in the wall side facing the bedroom. I didn't figure this out immediately, but when I found my pillowcases lettered with black chalk with titles such as "Mary greets her boyfriend". "John discoveries that his sister has grown up" and "Tonight's the Night". I finally figured out that they were making porno movies with the cameraman in the closet and the actors in the bed. I wondered if the two or more in the bed knew the cameraman was in the closet.

I took the next week off and with the help of the plumber I put the house back in a livable condition. I patched the holes in the closet walls, removed all the empty wine bottles, painted the walls, and replaced the furniture that was beyond repair, cleaned the carpets, put the glass back in the "French Doors" and changed the locks. I saved all the repair bills and kept track of the time it took to get the work done. While I was working on the house the mailman brought a letter from the young lady's husband who was in the service.

I copied his return address and sat down and wrote him a brief letter.

Dear Sgt. _____.

Your wife rented a house on the lake from me at the address where you sent this letter. She moved about a week ago and while I was cleaning the house to rent it again I

3

found several personal things of hers that I'm sure she would appreciate having returned. If you send me her forwarding address I will be glad to contact her and return the items.

Sincerely,

Guess what???? In about 2 weeks I received a nice letter from him thanking me for my concern and giving me her new address, which happened to be her mother's house. I added up all the repair bills and itemized them all on a statement for her. My sister and I drove over to the address he had given me.

We went up to the front door, rang the bell and stood back where we could not be seen from the inside. The door opened and there stood my former tenant. She was absolutely shocked to see me. I told her I would like to come in and discuss how she intended to pay me for the damages to my house. I lied and told her the lady with me was a social worker and would like to discuss the health and welfare of her baby who had been exposed to the conditions we discovered. I handed her the itemized bill and she looked at it briefly and said, "I can give you one half now and the other half in two weeks". I told her I'd agree to this. She ran to a back room and just about that time a car pulled in the driveway. It was her mother.

My former tenant came running out of the back room and started counting out the money to me – and in walked her mother. Her mother asked, "What's going on? And who is this, and why are you giving her all this money?" I introduced myself and said "I'm her former landlord of 3 months and she is paying for the damages to the house while she was living there."

Her mother said "I thought you were a friend of Mrs. _____ and were allowing her to live with you" I said, "Your daughter, her sister and her brother answered an ad in the paper under "Furnished house for rent" and she rented the house from me." Her mother said, "She doesn't have a sister or a brother". I said, "I'm only telling you what she told me. They were introduced as her sister and brother" I turned to the girl and said, "I expect to hear from you in two weeks." And we left.

Two weeks to the day I got a call from my former tenant and she told me she didn't have the balance of the money but would send it to me as she got it. I explained to her that I had written this nice letter to her husband and that's how I found out where she was living, however; if I didn't get the balance of the money in the next week I'd write to him again and really tell him the truth. I received a money order for the balance due within 3 days of our conversation.

CHAPTER 2

The Couple from Australia

A nice young couple made an appointment to see the one bedroom apartment I had in a "four unit" building I owned. They inspected the apartment and agreed that it was what they were looking for. They signed the "Rental Agreement" and paid the 1st month's rent. They asked for time to come up with the security and last month's rent. They said they'd have the balance by the time the next month's rent was due.

Everything was fine for almost a year and suddenly they had a falling out. It seems they fought every night after they came home from work. Everyone has a fight now and then so when the neighbors called and told me they were being kept up at night by these two fighting I went over to their apartment one evening to have a talk with them. I told them that I understood that they were having domestic problems. I told them that I'm sure many married couples go through times like this, but living in a 4-unit apartment causes more problems. It is summer and people have their windows open so it is necessary that they keep their windows closed and keep their voices down when they are fighting. I suggested that they go down to the beach or to a park to have their loud disagreements. Furthermore, I was told that on several occasions the wife came charging out the front door at 3:00 A.M., jumped into her car, turned on the headlights and went screeching down the street. The other tenants said when she turned on her headlights at that hour it was just like daylight in their front bedroom and that wasn't the end, the husband then ran out on the porch and in his loudest voice cursed, swore, and threatened as to what would happen if she returned. After a couple of these episodes everyone had enough.

I happened to catch them in a good mood when I talked to them and they assured me that they would get their problems straightened out and it wouldn't happen again. A couple weeks later one of my other tenants came to my house to pay his rent and told me that everything was very quiet for the past few days and he was sure she had left.

The Australian couple's rent was due and they did not show up to pay the rent so after three days I went over to see what was going on. I rapped on the front door and the lady in the building next door came to the window and said, "Mrs. X has left for good, but Mr. X said you shouldn't go in his apartment because he was coming back "

He might be coming back but his rent was past due, so I used my key to assess the situation. I discovered that all their personal items were gone, the closets were empty, and the few dirty dishes in the sink looked like they had been there for a week or so

It so happened that my son and daughter in-law were visiting at my house. When I went home and told them that I had a vacant apartment to clean, they volunteered to help. The three of us went back to the apartment to prepare it for the next rental. My daughter in-law agreed to start in the kitchen, usually the most time consuming.

I usually defrost the refrigerator and pull it away from the wall so I can clean underneath it. Now, this act alone is very interesting because behind and underneath the refrigerator I have found many things. I found bankbooks; check books, cookbooks, food (both liquid and solid), old newspapers, letters, silverware, and you name it. My daughter-in-law started in the kitchen and my son asked, "What would you like me to do?"

The apartment had a heater built in the wall that hadn't been used for years because all of the apartments now have reverse cycle air conditioners. I told him I would be very pleased to have that wall heater removed and a frame made for the opening with shelves to make a bookshelf. He took the front cover off and guess what??? My Australian friend had put three medium size raw fish inside the wall heater.

Within about 15 minutes my daughter in-law yelled from the kitchen that something was dripping in one of the lower cupboards. Two raw fish were lying on the lower shelf of the cupboard.

It was really a miracle that things worked out as they did and that I entered the apartment within a few days after the tenant left, also that my son was there and we decided to remove the wall heater. We are in Florida; this is a summer month, and an upstairs apartment. Within a few more days the odor and damage could have been tremendous.

For some unexplainable reason my tenant decided to punish me for his domestic problems. The neighbor next door had befriended them and told me that they were not married and were arguing about getting married. Seems she wanted to and he didn't. That was really none of my business and it didn't matter to me, so why the fish??? Did he think she was coming back? Was he punishing her or me???

CHAPTER 3

One child, fourteen cats and a dog

A young lady in her middle twenties came to rent a one-bedroom apartment in my duplex. She had a child about 4 years old. I try not to rent to anyone with children because this duplex is on a corner in a residential neighborhood and there is a lot of traffic on that corner and the yard is not fenced in. My past experience has been that small children are always looking for new experiences. I have had all the sprinkler heads unscrewed and removed from the sprinklers. the clock on the side of the house has had the switch turned on which let the sprinklers run for 48 hours resulting in a hefty water bill. Most of all, it's the traffic and an open yard.

This young lady told me she was a nurse who worked at one of our local hospitals. She said she would be working all day and her child would be at Nursery School all day and she would be picking him up at the end of the day. My heart made the decision to rent to her and I rented the apartment to her. She only had the first month's rent but said she would have the balance of the money due within a week. For 10 years I had been a widow with a small child and struggling

9

to support us both. I felt that maybe she needed a helping hand at this point in her life.

She forgot to tell me that she had two pregnant cats and a dog and they all moved in together. Within two weeks the two cats each had 6 kittens so she now had 14 cats, a dog and a small child in this one bedroom apartment.

After 10 days I went down to see if she had the balance of the money due for Security and Last month's rent. She was never there. At the end of three weeks I found out about all the cats. I learned from the tenant in the other end of the duplex that she didn't work during the day but frequently left the apartment about 10 P.M. and didn't return until 3:00 or 4:00 A.M. I was told that she didn't take the child with her but put him to bed before leaving.

I was now in the 4th week since I had seen her and I hadn't received any money toward the last month's rent and security. I made it a point to stop by the apartment morning, noon, and night until I found her home. When she opened the door I saw the cats, dog, and the child and smelled the house. The odor was sickening. I told her she would have to move because she had not been honest with me when she moved in regarding the animals. This is a furnished apartment and I was concerned for the furnishings with all these animals. I suggested that she take the animals to the Humane Society to find homes for them. She yelled at me and said she would have no part of that but would find adoptive homes for them all. She said she was trying every day. I told her she would have to move when the rent was up in three days. In fact, I went home and made out a 3 Days Notice to move.

Three days passed by and when I went down to see what was happening I found the pane in the front jalousie door had been removed and the screen in the front window was removed so she had a case hardened chain going through the front window and around through the front jalousie door with a padlock on it so nobody could get in. Unbelievable!!!

I looked through the front window and saw the animals and when they saw me they came to the window the cats were meowing and the dog was barking. I went back every three hours to see if she had returned because I was getting sick over the whole situation. It was very hot outside and what if she had left and abandoned the animals? I called the police and when they arrived I discussed the situation with them. The only advice they could legally give me was to go to court and file for an eviction. That could take 30 to 60 days and this situation didn't have that much time. I asked the police officer if he would just stand there while I went inside and rescued the animals. Bless his heart, he did. I took a hammer and broke the padlock and entered the apartment.

I had called two friends earlier in the day and told them about the situation. At this time I called them again and asked them to pick up some large boxes at the grocery store so we could put the animals in them and take them to the Humane Society. When we were inside picking up cats I noticed a dresser drawer half open and a revolver was lying inside. On the dresser were Credit Cards and a Gas Card made out in the name of a prominent man in Palm Beach. I wrote down his name and also the name of the motel and the room number on it.

Just about this time a car pulled up and the girl and her child came charging in. (and I do mean, "charging in". She screamed, swore, threatened and ordered us out. Thank goodness the officer was standing on the porch and probably prevented further violence. I told her I wanted her out immediately. Her rent was three days late and she had no money to pay next month's rent or the last month and security. I told her I would be back the next day and expected her to be gone.

I called the Motel where the key on her dresser was from. The manager extended his sympathy when I identified the lady and her son. He said they had stayed at his motel for two months free and when he started proceedings to evict them she took a knife and slashed the furniture, drapes and even the carpet. He advised me to be careful because he felt she could be dangerous. Needless to say, I didn't sleep very well that night.

I went to the apartment the next day and told her I had talked to the motel manager where she had stayed before coming to this apartment and I was going to stay right there in her living room until she left and she had better not damage anything while getting out. She had all her clothes in green garbage bags, which she kept in the bathtub. She started carrying out her clothes and animals and was gone by noon.

From some of the papers and correspondence left behind I determined that she was the mistress of a prominent socialite in Palm Beach and could have been a maid in his home. The child she had was probably his and he was supporting her. The times she left at night were probably times when she met with him.

CHAPTER 4

A Mom Tries to Straighten Out Her Son

The "For Rent" sign was out in the yard again when I got a call from a woman who said she would like to meet me to view the apartment. She drove up in a Cadillac and was very well dressed. I was surprised that she was looking for a one-bedroom apartment in a duplex, although the duplex is in a nice residential upper middle class neighborhood. I met her and she walked through the apartment and seemed well pleased.

We sat down in the living room and she explained that she was looking for an apartment for her son who was in his middle thirties and was presently staying with her and his father. He had been living with a divorcee and her three children in a neighboring state. They had an argument and the girl threw him out, so when he arrived at her home he had nothing but his clothes in a suitcase. He was well educated and had a good job but his money had all been spent on this woman and her three children. The mother felt that this girl was absolutely "trash" and had just used him for his money.

He begged his mother and dad to help him get started again in the right direction. They had already bought him a car and he had found a good job in this area. All he needed was a furnished apartment and his life would be off to a new start. She paid the 1st month's rent, security and the last month's rent so everything was set up for him to move in.

Within about three weeks a broken down car arrived pulling a trailer. His former girlfriend and her three small children moved in this one bedroom apartment. Of course, his mother had signed an Agreement which stated that there would be One adult and No children occupying the apartment.

I called his mother and told her that there were five people occupying the apartment and this was not acceptable to me. She broke down and cried and said that he had called his former girlfriend and they patched up their differences so he invited her and the children to join him here in Florida. He told his mother that he couldn't live without her. I told the mother that they could not stay and she would have to find them another place to live. She told me to tell them myself because she wasn't speaking to him.

I went to the apartment in the evening after he got home from work and they had time to eat their dinner. I rapped on the door and when he answered I asked if I could come in and talk to him. He let me in and what I saw made me sick. The kids had been sleeping on the couch and floor in the living room. There was food on every table and soda bottles sitting everywhere (some were full and some were half empty). Everything I could see pointed to "Fast Food-carry out". There were dried up pieces of pizza on the arm of a chair, Burger King bags and boxes strewn throughout the room, and half eaten Kentucky Colonel Chicken dinners on the sink and kitchen table. I saw at least $50.00 worth of Florida souvenirs – T shirts on the floor, pictures of dolphins, Mickey Mouse, Disney castle, rubber alligators, miniature fruit trees to plant, etc. It looked like they had stopped at Disney land on their way down here.

We had a discussion about the condition of the apartment and the fact that the rental agreement stated there would only be one person living there. He defended their actions and said they intended to stay and live out the last month's rent that his mother had paid. I explained again that the last month's rent was for the 12th month, not the 2nd month of a one-year agreement. It was not his decision to decide which month was the last month. He told me to get out of the apartment.

Because I was furnishing the electric and water, I called up the next morning and had the electric turned off. I would have turned off the water but the entire building only had one meter. The next night when I drove by I saw an extension cord running across the front porch from their apartment to the one next door. The next day I confronted the next-door neighbor regarding the extension cord and he told me he felt sorry for them and allowed them to run an extension cord from his apartment to theirs. When I drove by the building the next evening they were all sitting out on the front porch together having a good time. The adults each had a bottle of beer in their hands and the children were each holding a bag of popcorn.

I went back a couple nights later after they had been there for about 5 weeks. I told them that I was going to change the locks on the front and back door so they better get their things out the next day. (Of course, the law doesn't allow me to do this, but I had to put some fear in them). I was using any threat I could think of to save my furniture and apartment from further damage. They were now afraid to leave the apartment for fear that I would change the locks. The mother and kids had been spending the day at the beach where the kids enjoyed the ocean. When I drove by the apartment the next evening, they were carrying out bags of clothes etc. and loading them in the trailer. I hoped they had found a larger apartment and I would never see them again.

Sometime the next day they vacated the apartment and I got a call from the son asking for the Security and last month's rent refund. I explained that I had not had time to inspect the apartment and if he would leave me his forwarding address I would decide if they had any money coming. He said he'd call me in a few days and pick up the money.

The next morning I got a call from the mother who had rented the apartment from me originally. She reminded me that she had given me a personal check when she rented the apartment and if there was any refund it was to be given to her. She had driven by the apartment and knew that they had left.

I went to the apartment to assess the damage and prepare it to rent again. I discovered that the mother of the children (or maybe the adults) had used the toilet for bowel movements and not flushed the toilet, but she then poured at least two large hands full of shells on top. I could not flush the toilet because the shells would have caused untold damage to the plumbing. I had to get rubber gloves and dip out the toilet by hand. The security was used up cleaning up the apartment and replacing sheets, towels and pots and pans, which they took with them.

The son called me again a few days later and was furious when I told him that he would not be getting any money for two reasons. First, it was his mother's money that had rented the apartment and 2nd because the cleanup and damage had eaten up the balance. He was furious because he thought he would get that out of his mother too.

CHAPTER 5

A Father Reunites With His Son

I had my two-bedroom furnished apartment for rent and got a call on a Saturday morning from a man who would like to see the apartment. I met him at l0:00 A.M. and he liked the apartment and said he would like to rent it and would sign a One year agreement. He wrote me a check for first, last and security and then told me that his son would be living with him and sharing the apartment. His son was 15 years old. School is within walking distance so I anticipated no serious problems.

When he got up to leave he said he was going to the Ft. Lauderdale airport to pick up his son. The plane was arriving at one o'clock and he was nervous because he hadn't seen the boy in four years. He and his wife had divorced and she had custody of their son. His wife had been in contact with him recently and told him she was having problems with the boy. She felt he was too much for her to handle so they agreed to have him live with his father for a year.

They moved in together and seemed to be making it OK because I heard of no problems. I heard from the neighbors that the boy had befriended another boy at school.

Apparently the other boy was having problems at home and had run away. My tenant's son was allowing his friend to sleep in the storage shed at the rear of the building. My tenant was not aware of this until the friend's parents followed him home from school to see where he was hanging out. I guess the two boys came home from school and ate together but instead of going home at 10:00 o'clock he went back to the storage shed and spent the night. The friend's parents called the police and they discovered what had been going on. I felt sorry for the friend who had been sleeping in the shed but I was glad the situation had been resolved and he was back home. I guess that was the end of it because the neighbor said he hadn't been around any more.

I got a call once that the plumbing was plugged up and the toilet wouldn't flush. I called the plumber and he dug out paper towels that had been used when the toilet paper ran out. My tenant was very understanding and paid the plumbing bill. It was something any of our kids probably would have done in an emergency.

The day that the lease was up, the father put the boy on a plane and sent him back to his mother. Maybe the boy had changed after living with his dad for a year. I hope it was a pleasant experience for both of them and that he and his mother get along better. I never heard from them again.

CHAPTER 6

A Real Gentleman

Two young men showed up to look at my one bedroom furnished apartment. One was looking for an apartment and the other was driving him around to see what was available.

The one who was looking for an apartment said he had just arrived from Atlanta and thanks to his friend he already had a job at a local bank in the mortgage department. It was the bank his friend worked at. They were college graduates and had known each other at college.

I kidded him and asked if he knew how to keep house. He assured me that he had lived 4 years in the college dorm and had kept house there. I told him that didn't count because I had visited my son in college and saw how they kept house. We both laughed and he gave me the required money to rent for a year.

The application to rent required a reference and he listed the friend he was with. It so happened that the bank where he was going to work was the same bank that I dealt with. When I went to make a deposit the next day I casually asked the girl at the information desk, " Does Mr. X work

20

here? " She got up and said, "Please follow me". I found myself in the office of my new tenant and a sign on his desk identifying him as one of the Vice Presidents. When he came back to his office I told him "I didn't come here for a visit, I just wanted to confirm that you worked here". We both laughed and I bowed out.

He lived in my apartment for seven years and about once a month he invited one of his girlfriends over for the weekend. She cleaned the kitchen, did the laundry and cleaned the apartment. I guess his girlfriends were many because I saw a lot of different cute girls on weekends.

One day he called and asked me to stop by and look at the front of his refrigerator. He said the paint had come off. I stopped and looked at his refrigerator and sure enough, up and down the whole front side the paint was off down to the bare steel. I asked him what he was using to clean the front and he turned and picked up a Brillo pad lying on the sink. That answered my question. I suggested that he use a sponge and soapy water in the future.

I asked him to roll the refrigerator out on the porch on the next Saturday morning and I bought a couple spray cans of white appliance spray paint. After taping the handle and hinges I sprayed the front door of the refrigerator and it looked like new. He was very pleased.

Another time he called because the kitchen faucet was dripping. I went over while he was working and put in a new washer and just by luck I opened the oven door. There was at least ½" of grease on the bottom of the oven. I got a putty knife out of my toolbox, scraped up the bulk of the grease, and with paper towels I wiped out the rest of it. I went to the store and bought a can of oven cleaner and came back and cleaned the sides and burnt spots. It cleaned up like a new oven.

That evening I called him and asked "How do you broil your meat in the oven?" He said he just laid the meat on the oven shelf for 5 minutes on each side. That answered the question as to where all the grease came from. I told him he had to use a broiler pan and that he was just lucky that he didn't have a fire in the oven from all the grease.

This is the same man who volunteered to trim the huge Christmas tree in the bank lobby.

He told me that he strung all the lights on the tree and had to use a ladder to reach the top. When he wound the last string of lights around the top, he discovered that at the end of the string of lights he was holding was the plug that should have been plugged into the wall at the bottom to light the tree.

He was a very good tenant but was just not a housekeeper. When he left at the end of 7 years he had advanced to Bank Manager at another branch. He was always well dressed and a perfect gentleman and I was sorry to see him go.

CHAPTER 7

The Taxi Driver

I rented a furnished room to a young man who drove a taxi. He was a nice person in every way. He dressed neatly, had a good vocabulary and was very polite.

One evening a couple that lived in the apartment next door to him came to my house to pay their rent. They were playing with my new puppy and making light conversation when one of them said, "By the way, we heard water running all afternoon in the room next door to our apartment, and as we were leaving to come over here there was a trickle of water coming out of the front door of that room ".

I couldn't believe that they were so unconcerned about what I considered an emergency situation. I told them they'd have to come back at another time to play with the puppy because I was leaving immediately to go over and see what had happened.

I got in my car and drove over to the apartment building and sure enough, water was coming out from under the front door of the hotel room. I used my passkey to get in because obviously the taxi driver wasn't home. When I opened the front door I saw at least 1" of water covering the entire floor of the back bedroom and living room. The danger in this case could be from extension cords lying bare on the floor. I tested the water, took off my shoes, rolled up my slacks and headed for the bathroom where the water had to be coming from. I could hear the toilet running. I took the back off the top of the toilet tank and discovered a defective flush valve was allowing the water to rise to the level of the flush handle, and at that level the water could run out the hole where the flush handle was attached. The hole for the flush handle was larger than was necessary, and there was a lot of space for the water to just run down the front of the toilet tank.

I turned the water off and drove down to the drug store where I rented a "rinse 'n vac" rug cleaner. I only needed the attachment that sucks up the excess water. I came back with the "rinse 'n vac" and picked up my grandson who lives a few blocks away.

I started sucking up the water while he carried out the tables, chairs, lamps, and other light furniture. There's no way we could drag the carpet out with the weight of all that water on it so we had to wait until we had sucked up as much water as possible and then we pulled the carpet out on the patio to dry. When we pulled the carpet outside I discovered $300.00 under the corner of the carpet. I dried out the money on a bath towel and put it in a dresser drawer. Inside the dresser drawer I saw a bankbook with $800.00 in a savings account. I was very happy to see that he was doing so well.

When the floor was dry we carried all the furniture back in the apartment and I left a note on the outside of the front door. The note said to call me when he got home and that everything is under control. I figured he'd be shook up when he pulled up in front of the building and saw the carpet spread out on the patio soaking wet and remembering that he had hid money underneath it. He called later and

I explained what had happened and where I put the wet money I found. I had replaced the flush valve so it was just a matter of drying the carpet and getting it back the next day. We were in luck because the sun came out the next day and dried the top of the carpet. I went back over there in the afternoon and turned the carpet over and dried the backside. My grandson came over there in the evening and we put the room back together.

Everything seemed to be going well for the taxi driver until Thanksgiving rolled around. I guess the pressure of being alone for the holiday and thinking about Christmas just around the corner was too much for him. He started on a drinking binge Thanksgiving Day. He paid his rent on December 1st but that was the last time. He drank up all his cash reserve and drew all the money out of the bank and drank that up too. Of course, he lost his job.

January 1st rolled around and he didn't have any money to pay his rent. I stopped by his room to see how he was doing and he looked terrible. He hadn't shaved and there were empty bottles sitting on the floor. There were cigarettes and filled cigarette ashtrays sitting on the tables and on the floor. I talked to him and reminded him how well he had been doing and how happy I was when I saw that he had a savings account and had been able to buy himself some really nice shirts and slacks. His closet was filled with nice clothes.

He told me he hadn't eaten for two days because he didn't have any money. I made a mistake by giving him ten dollars. Looking back, I should have gone to the store and bought him a couple hamburgers and milk shake because he probably spent the money on more alcohol. I begged him to stop drinking and get himself back in shape. He promised that he would stop drinking and would look for another job.

He needed help but I wasn't trained to say and do what was needed to help him.

I stopped by about every other day to see what progress he was making. By this time his rent was a couple weeks past due. Each time instead of collecting rent I gave him a few dollars to buy food and tried to encourage him to clean himself up and look for a job. He didn't have a car and one time when I stopped by another man was there drinking with him. His friend might have been living there too, I didn't know. Finally, in desperation I told him he'd have to move out so I could clean up the room and rent it. He agreed. I asked him if he had any relatives in this area that could help him get back on his feet. He said he had a grandmother living in the next city that was about ten miles from where he was now living. I asked him for her name and address and went home and called her.

I told her the sad story and asked her if she would help her grandson until he got back on his feet. She told me she had her own problems and had just gotten out of the hospital and didn't want him around drinking. I begged her to give him another chance but she said absolutely not.

I went back to his hotel room and my tenant was just sitting there not knowing how to get started. I asked him if he had a suitcase to put his clothes in but he didn't. I suggested that he put his clothes in a green plastic garbage bag so they wouldn't get wet or lost and he agreed. I gave him a couple green garbage bags and he started packing. It was heart breaking.

I asked him about his family and he said his parents had divorced years before and he was an only child. He said his mother was an alcoholic and had remarried but he didn't have any idea where she was living. After he filled the two garbage bags with what he wanted to take he left on foot with the two garbage bags over his shoulder. This was not the man who had rented the room originally. This was a completely different person.

I spent the next couple days cleaning and painting the room and doing the laundry. Most of the bed linens have to be discarded after they have been slept in for long periods without being laundered. They absorb the body oil and sweat, and tear easily. I bought new bed linens and towels. The towels had been used to mop up the floor after he threw up, so they had to be all replaced. Towels and bed linens aren't cheap anymore. I can easily spend $100.00 for replacements. I got the room back in good condition and had a new tenant in a few days.

He had left 5 or 6 new shirts and several pair of new slacks in the closet so I put them in another garbage bag and threw them in the trunk of my car. I intended to take them to the Salvation Army in the next week or so.

A few nights later my son and grandchildren were over to my house for the evening. We were talking about taking a trip up North so I mentioned that I had a road map in the glove compartment of my car. I asked one of the kids to get it from my car in the car -port. One of the kids, the 15 year old, ran out the back door but returned in a flash and quickly slammed the door shut and locked it. He was as white as a sheet and we all inquired what had happened. He said, "There's a man in your car port". My son jumped up and ran for the back door with all of us behind him. There stood my former tenant the taxi driver. My son didn't know who he was and asked, "Who are you and what do you want?" I recognized him and immediately said, "That's my former tenant who just moved."

He stood there with a beard wearing the same clothes he had on when he left his room. He said he had lost all of his clothes and wondered if I had found any in his closet and if I still had them. I told my son that some of his clothes were still in a green garbage bag in my trunk and I went back in the house to get the keys to my trunk. I unlocked the trunk and handed him $5.00 at the same time. My son got the garbage bag out of the trunk and handed it to him. He also told him he didn't ever want to catch him around my house again. He took his clothes and left and I've never seen him since. When we all got back in the house my son said "He looked like he hadn't eaten for a week so I gave him $5.00". I said, "So did I".

CHAPTER 8

Aware Of Constant Maintenance

Finding furniture and carpets within an affordable price range is an art in itself. I have several friends who own rental property and we all do the same thing. We read the want ads and try to find good furniture from them. We also check the consignment shops and the garage sales. Broyhill Furniture Co. had a warehouse in our area for many years where they sold new and used rental furniture. When the furniture was returned after the rental period, it was put on sale. I purchased like-new rental furniture, at a very good price.

My friend and I laid carpet in 7 rooms one fall. We bought remnants from a carpet warehouse. We carry our room sizes with us at all times when we are looking for carpet so we were always ready to catch a bargain. We have wall-to-wall carpets in every room but we don't fasten the carpet to nailed strips around the edges. If the room is perfectly rectangular we can turn the carpet around when it starts to show path marks or wear. We use double seal tape where two pieces of carpet meet. We buy vinyl tile for the kitchen and bathroom and lay it ourselves. We have ceiling fans in almost every room and install them ourselves. We do almost all repair work ourselves except for major plumbing jobs.

We are constantly updating. All my apartments are in excellent condition and I feel that I could live in any apartment and be comfortable. I ask my tenants to immediately report any problems that come up. Very few problems improve by themselves. They only get worse with time.

If a faucet drips I get there as soon as possible and replace the washer or seat. If the toilet is running I want to know as soon as possible so it can be taken care of before the water bill goes up. If the air conditioner isn't blowing out cold air, I need to know it, so I can have it checked. Everything should be operating properly at all times. I think everyone feels comfortable with the rules and our service and they have said this on many occasions.

When my husband and I purchased a four-unit building, while talking to the former owners who were husband and wife, she said, "I told my husband that I'm not cleaning after anyone and when a tenant moves out he will have to hire a cleaning company to clean it for the next tenant." That's exactly what happened, and after a few years he decided that they weren't making any money on their rentals so they put the property up for sale. It would not have been profitable for us if we had to hire out all the clean up when tenants move. My husband was an office worker all his life and did not adapt to being a landlord, so I took over all the management of our property. Very shortly after we bought the property my husband died so managing the apartments worked out as we had planned. I continued renting the apartments when tenants moved and doing most of the clean up, minor repairs and painting. My son and two grandsons were always willing to help when I called them. I am in good health and I took it all in stride. It worked for me. We were not "big time" land- owners. It was enough to keep me busy. I am getting older so am now down to owning only four rental units. I have a lot of good memories and then there are the ones I have written about. I was never bored with my life because besides the rentals I own, I also own and live in a three -bedroom home that takes up a lot of my time.

I strongly recommend rental property as an investment but you have to have patience and be aware of what's going on at all times, at each place, in order to make money. Rental property in Florida is probably different from the Northern cities because we have such a big turnover. Many come down here to work in the winter because of the weather. They come down with nothing but their clothes in the back of their car. Service jobs are always in demand during the season, but then so many people go back North for the summer that things are a lot quieter after the "season". Waiters and waitresses sometimes have a hard job keeping their bills paid after the winter visitors leave and things quiet down. I've rented to some. But – It worked for me and it can for you too.

CHAPTER 9

Dead Tenant

I rented a one bedroom apartment to an elderly gentleman who had lived in the area years ago and returned because he liked the climate and liked to walk the sandy beaches in the morning. He had a nice car, one year old, and seemed to be financially independent.

He lived in the apartment approximately 8 months when I got a call from the tenant at the other end of the building. She asked me where I was all afternoon during the excitement. I had been out visiting a friend most of the afternoon so I wasn't around.

She proceeded to tell me what happened. Apparently my tenant had met a lady on the beach and they struck up a conversation. They discovered that they each lived alone and decided it would be nice to have dinner together occasionally. They had dinner together a few times, each paying for their own dinner.

The lady drove by his apartment, saw his car parked by the house, so stopped by to see if he wanted to go out for dinner later. She rang the bell but there was no answer. She peeked through the window and could see him lying on the floor in the doorway between the bathroom and the bedroom. She called the police and they called the emergency squad. In a few minutes the area was swarming with police and ambulances. They had to break a window to get in because the tenant at the other end of the building tried to call me for a key, but I was not home.

When they got inside they discovered that he had been dead for about 12 hours. He died while sitting on the toilet and then fell forward. I later found out that it is not uncommon for elderly people to die sitting on the toilet and straining too much.

I had to call his son who lived out of state. He made all funeral arrangements and I told him any family members could stay in his father's apartment when they came down to pick up his car and other personal items. They did come down and stay there. I had to help them identify what things were his and what was furnished with the apartment. It was a sad ending.

CHAPTER 10

Girls From The Strip Tease Club

I had three apartments vacant at the same time, one next to the other in a three-unit duplex. There's a full one-bedroom apartment at each end of the duplex and an efficiency apartment in the middle. I got a call from a young lady who wanted to rent an apartment. She liked the efficiency apartment and said she would be back with two more friends who all worked at the same place. They wanted to live close to each other because they went back and forth to work in a taxi and that saved them money to ride together. She came back a short time later and rented the efficiency. She told me her friend Betty was on her way over and wanted to rent one of the other apartments. She said they were waitresses at a Striptease Club at the edge of the city. Looking back, I now believe all three of them were strip tease dancers.

In a short time Betty arrived and a young man in an orange Volkswagen pulled up behind her. She introduced herself and then introduced her friend and added, "This is my new friend who I met about a week ago." She added, "It just seemed like a series of coincidences the way we kept running into each other after we first met. We ran into each other at the shopping center, then at Denny's restaurant where I stopped to eat, then at the beach. It seemed like every place I went, he showed up."

She rented the apartment but only gave me the 1st month's rent. She said she would have the balance of the money in about a week. I trusted her. After about a week her new found boyfriend decided to go back to Chicago where he said he had lived. Believe it or not – she decided to go to Chicago with him. I knew that she had only known him for a total of two weeks. So many girls around the country disappear. I worried about her decision to accompany a man to another state after only knowing him for such a short period of time. I never heard any more about her.

Several days after the first girl rented the apartment the third girl showed up at my house. She probably got my address from her girl friend. She said she had seen her friend's apartment and wanted to rent the other vacant apartment. This girl who I'll call "Sandy" looked very young to me. She was a beautiful girl. She had blond hair and looked like she had just come from the beauty shop. She had blue eyes and beautiful ivory skin. I asked her how old she was and she told me she was 16 years old. I told her I couldn't rent an apartment to her because she was too young to sign a rental agreement. I kidded her and added that another reason was because I didn't want the neighbors complaining about boyfriends running in and out of her apartment. She had a roll of money in her hand to pay me before I told her that she was too young to sign a contract and I couldn't rent to her. I could see that she had all her clothes in her car when she pulled up. She left after our conversation.

About three hours later, a Mercedes pulled up in front of my house. A man who appeared to be in his mid thirties accompanied the same blond young lady. They came in and the man gave me his business card and showed me his driver's license. He told me he was her Fiancée and he would rent the apartment and be responsible for both the apartment and her behavior. Apparently she told him what I had said because he said he didn't want men running in and out of the apartment either.

They said they were planning on getting married in the next year but at the present time he was working out of town. Within a year he expected to be back in town permanently. When he got back they would buy a house and get married. It sounded reasonable to me so I rented him the apartment knowing that she would be living there. What neither he or I knew at that time was that she was 2 months pregnant and had no idea who the father was.

She was a nude dancer at the Strip Tease Club, so after 3 months her body began to reveal her situation and she was fired. When I drove by the building where she was living I noticed that all the blinds were down on all the windows. I stopped by the building one morning to talk to her friend in the middle apartment.

She said she was very concerned about her friend, Sandy, and feared that she might be contemplating suicide. By this time her Fiancée had recognized the situation and had left her. I went to the apartment to talk to her. She answered the door and I told her I would like to come in and talk to her because I felt she might need help. I inquired about family or friends who could help. She was an only child and her parents lived in Atlanta. I strongly advised her to contact her mother. Her situation was only going to get worse. In desperation she later contacted her mother who came down to see her. By this time she was 5 months pregnant.

The next news I heard was from her friend who lived next door. She told me Sandy was on both alcohol and drugs when she got pregnant and had no idea who was the father of the baby. She and her mother were afraid the baby would be affected so her mother arranged for a private abortion. She left the apartment and I never saw her again. However, her friend told me later that she was back at the Strip Tease Club dancing about 2 months after the abortion.

During my conversation with my tenant I learned that it was very important that their address be kept secret from their customers. Their customers had no respect for them and that's why they took a taxi to and from work. She said once any of their regular customers found out where they lived the "guys" would show up at their residence any time of the day or night and make it impossible for them to continue living at that address.

After a few months my tenant disappeared -- and I really mean, "disappeared". I hadn't seen her for about a week, and when she didn't come to pay her rent, I went to her apartment to see if she was O.K. She didn't answer the door so I used my key to enter the apartment. From all indication she left suddenly. There were several pans and a frying pan on the stove with food in them. It looked like she was cooking a meal when she picked up and left. Her clothes were gone and it was a mystery to me as to what had happened.

I never found out if she left voluntarily or if someone appeared suddenly and forced her out of the apartment with him or her. I watched the paper for several weeks but nothing in the paper ever gave me a clue. I didn't feel that I knew her well enough to make a "missing person report" because she could have just packed up and gone back home or moved to another address. I hope this is what happened.

CHAPTER 11

A Sister And Two Brothers

I had two apartments vacant at this time. One was on the first floor and the other was on the second floor directly above. The apartment on the first floor was a two-bedroom apartment and the one on the 2nd floor was a one-bedroom apartment.

I received a call from a lady who made an appointment for her and her husband to meet me and see one apartment. They liked the upstairs apartment and made a deposit on it. She told me that she had two brothers who lived in the area and she had been doing their housework and laundry, and it certainly would be more convenient if they all lived in the same building. She said she'd talk to them and get back in contact with me. The next day I received a call from one of the brothers who identified himself and made an appointment to see the two-bedroom apartment.

Both the sister and her brothers were well dressed, had clean new cars and said they all had good jobs. This was true. They signed a rental agreement, paid 1st, last, and security and moved in. Shortly thereafter, I found out that every Friday night all four of them started drinking and continued drinking during the entire weekend.

One morning I passed by the building and saw that every jalousie glass in the front door was missing. That evening I stopped by to inquire what happened. They told me the wind had caught the door and it swung back against the mailbox and all the jalousies got broken. Well, this was a far-fetched story but they told me they had hired a glass company to come out the next day and replace all the jalousies. Sure enough, they did.

Several months later when I drove by the building I noticed the front awning that shaded the 9 ft. picture window. was dropped down against the building. They came to my house to pay their rent and I asked why the awning had been dropped. I was told that due to the fact that the front window faced West, the room was much cooler when the awning was dropped, thus blocking the sun. The building was about 16 years old and. up to that time nobody else had found it necessary to drop the awning to keep the room cool. Up to now, everyone else had been comfortable with the air conditioner running during the summer months, but if they wanted to try something different it wasn't hurting anyone so I let it pass.

Within a few months the sister decided to leave her husband and go back to her boyfriend. She didn't tell me when she rented the apartment that she and her husband had been separated for 2 years and were going to try to reconcile and make a go of their marriage. Apparently, it didn't work.

Her brothers were "out of control" on week ends after she left. The husband who now lived alone upstairs realized that he had to get separated from this situation. He came to my house to discuss the problems and asked if he could break the lease and go back to Atlanta where he had been living before he came down to reconcile with his wife. I told him I would allow him to break the lease. He then told me he needed the security deposit to make the trip back to Atlanta. He said he would call me to inspect the apartment after he had all his belongings in the car and was ready to leave. Reluctantly I agreed. This was a "big mistake" on my part. It really requires more than a walk thru to determine if everything is in workable and rental condition. The apartment appeared to be neat and tidy and I gave him cash from his security deposit.

When he was leaving he said, "There's a few things I want to tell you before I leave. First, when all the glass was broken out of the front jalousie door, it was because one of the brothers knocked the other right through the glass when they were drinking and fighting. Second, when they dropped the front awning. It was because they had a couple friends visiting them on Saturday afternoon and they were all sitting in the living room drinking. One of the men had a pulley on a string and he kept swinging it in a circle while they were sitting there idly talking and joking. Suddenly the pulley wore through the string and went straight through the front picture window. They paid $300.00 to have the glass replaced but while they were waiting to get their money together they dropped the front awning."

He also told me that I would find two bullet holes in the ceiling of the downstairs living room. He was right. I did find them. He continued to tell me that he had been downstairs and they were all drinking. They got into an argument so he left and went upstairs. He said when he got upstairs he was deliberately banging around and making unnecessary noise. They were annoyed and wanted him to know it so they got out their .22 and shot two holes in the ceiling. Fortunately the ceiling was so thick and dense that the bullets just lodged there and didn't go all the way through.

After he told me what had gone on downstairs he got in his car and left. A couple days later I went to his apartment to inspect it more carefully and prepare it for a rental. The coffee table was standing on four legs, three were attached and one was just propped carefully in place to give the appearance of being attached. When I pushed the table, the leg fell out from underneath. When I lifted the arm covers on the large upholstered chair I discovered that one had a 4-inch hole burnt in it. It's a wonder the chair didn't catch on fire.

When the two men moved from the downstairs apartment at the end of the year I discovered that the steel frame on one end of the twin bed was propped up by two bricks. It almost seems impossible to break the support off a steel frame that holds a caster. It certainly didn't break off by just sleeping in the bed. But it was broken.

CHAPTER 12

The Burned Out College Graduate

While I was cleaning a vacant apartment I placed my "For Rent" sign in the front yard. A couple people stopped by to inquire about the rent and then Freddie and his mother stopped by.

Freddie was a college graduate I was told, but he had a problem with drugs a few years back and now he was holding a low level job assembling lamps at a local wholesale lamp company.

I had just purchased new drapes for the bedroom and they were lying out on the bed ready to be hung. I was working in the bedroom and continued working while I was talking to them. Freddie sat on the drapes while we were talking. His mother was very patient and said to him, "Freddie, dear, you're sitting on the drapes." It would have been funny if I hadn't been annoyed.

She rented the apartment for him. She told me she would be paying the rent every month. She had remarried and it was more convenient to have Freddie living in his own apartment. She paid the rent and probably paid for the car he was driving.

Anytime I appeared on the premises, Freddie came out and wanted to talk to me. He appeared to be very lonesome. He bragged about how many different kinds of drugs he had tried and used. It was hard for him to hold a conversation very long. He was easily distracted and had a hard time concentrating. I heard from other tenants that he walked around his apartment yelling and crying at times. It seemed to get worse after a few months.

The neighbor next door told me Freddie would bring several chairs outside and then stand in front of them and talk. It was like he was lecturing to an unseen audience. They felt uneasy having him living there. One time I drove by and noticed that he had left his car lights on.

I Knocked on his door and told him his car lights were on. The explanation I got was "That's because I'm taking a shower and my favorite T.V. program is coming on in a few minutes." I told him to go and turn off the lights and then take his shower and watch his program. I didn't quite follow his conversation.

Freddie seemed to have a lot of minor problems in his apartment, especially with one wall plug that was controlled by a wall switch. He would plug the vacuum into this particular plug and unless the wall switch turned on the power, he could not start his vacuum. When this happened he would attempt to take the vacuum apart and fix it. He also tried to plug other appliances into that plug when it was turned off, and they all ended up by being taken apart. No matter how many times I tried to explain the connection between the wall switch and the plug it never registered with him.

Freddie's condition seemed to deteriorate and finally his mother picked him up and took him to a clinic for help.

She later came and took his clothes and that was the last I saw of Freddie. I felt bad for both of them. He was a very nice young man but had apparently burned his brain out on drugs.

CHAPTER 13

The Perfect Tenant

The sign outside reads "Furnished Apartment for Rent" so I received a call from a young man to see the apartment. He drove a nice new car that was clean and had no dents or bangs, which I always observe as I approach the building. He was well dressed and very polite. He filled out an application with the usual questions and during our conversation he mentioned that his mother lived a few blocks away in an expensive condominium. He had a very good job in a supervisory position and was just bouncing off a messy divorce. He liked the apartment and gave me a check. He planned on renting for a few years and then deciding if he wanted to buy a house or condominium. I thought I had found the "ideal tenant". Everything went smooth for the first year and then he renewed the lease for another year.

When I drove by the building one afternoon I noticed a cat sleeping in the window. I have no objections to an "in house, declawed cat" because I have two cats myself, but his lease reads, "there will be no animal without the consent of the landlord". I stopped by one evening when I saw his car in the driveway. A young lady answered the door and he was behind her. He introduced her as his long time girlfriend who was temporarily staying with him. I can go along with that because I try to avoid as many confrontations as possible. The cat was not declawed but she said she was going to have it done and it was being treated for fleas. Treating animals for fleas is a big "must" in Florida. We have warm weather 12 months a year so the fleas just keep multiplying. She was a waitress and had found a job within walking distance of the apartment.

The last week of the month they had a big fight and this was just a week before the rent was due. She called the police and had him arrested and he went to jail. The next morning I heard from one of the other tenants about the big fight.

When I stopped by the next day to see what had happened she told me he was in jail and the lease was in his name so it was his responsibility to pay the rent. His mother called me later that day and told me she had paid for his bail and he was at her house. She said he had to appear before a judge in 5 days but not to worry because it would all get straightened out and he would be calling me.

He appeared before the judge and his girlfriend got a "restraining order" keeping him away from her and the apartment for 90 days. So where does that leave me? The lease is in his name and he can't come near the place.

I went there to discuss this with her. She gave me the same "song and dance". She told me the lease was in his name and she didn't have enough money to pay the rent, and furthermore, she didn't intend to pay it so I could take her to court to get her evicted and that would probably take 3 or 4 months. I left her apartment and went straight to the courthouse to file for an eviction. The sheriff served her the papers after about 2 weeks and she had 10 days to answer. That process ate up the last month's rent that he had paid when he moved in.

The day before we were to appear in court she called me and asked me to come to the apartment and talk to her. She said she would be moving within 10 days. She had found a place but it wasn't ready for her to occupy yet. The new landlord was cleaning and painting it before it would be ready to move in.

The tenant next door told me that she was having a party every night with a lot of drinking and loud music so I knew what to expect when she left. It would cost me more money to go through with the eviction than it would to wait out the 10 days. She didn't move in 10 days but stayed for the entire month.

After she moved I went over and got it ready for a new tenant. My original tenant was now living with his mother and said he was not coming back because he had to repay his mother for the bail and also pay a lawyer that he hired and he was now in a bind for money.

When his girlfriend left she took all the dishes and flatware from the kitchen together with the sheets, towels and pillowcases. By the time I replaced what was missing and cleaned the apartment, my tenants security deposit was used up. I pay the electricity for the building so it cost me a 3-month electric bill plus the aggravation and clean up.

CHAPTER 14

A mother and child

Through the years I have found that renting to single men has given me less trouble. Single girls bring in their boyfriends and the boyfriends have no respect for my furnishings or property and the girls have a hard time controlling the situation.

Against my better judgment I rented a two-bedroom apartment to a woman and her daughter. She informed me that she would not be living in the apartment but that her daughter and grandson would occupy the apartment. She would be paying the rent every month. The daughter and her husband had just divorced and she needed help to get back on her feet.

It all sounded OK except that the daughter had a drinking problem and there is a local bar about 4 blocks away. I found out that she put the child to bed at 8 or 9 o'clock every night and then headed for the bar.

To complicate matters her ex-husband visited them and stayed several weekends. When he apparently found out about his ex-wife's going to the bar and picking up men and bringing them home, they got into a terrible fight and he knocked her through two of the louvered closet doors in the bedroom, knocking out all the louvers, so she ran into the bathroom and he kicked a hole in the bathroom door.

She had him arrested, so after that "he" was not the problem, but the men she brought home from the bar were. One time, two men at her house got into a fight and the police were called. Another time a man who owned a SUV parked in the driveway and was selling drugs until a neighbor observed the action and called the police.

I stopped by and discussed these problems with her and told her she'd have to move if it continued. Of course none of it was her fault. (I didn't know about the damaged doors until she moved) There was a smooth top stove in the kitchen and she asked me who to call for repairs. I had the bill of sale so I gave her the information, and I found out later that she had stepped on the top of the stove to reach the upper cupboard and had cracked the top of the stove. Her mother ordered a new stove at a cost of $450.00, which I found out about later.

During a fight with one of her boyfriends she ran in the bedroom and locked the door. Instead of going home, the boyfriend kicked in the bedroom door and even tore out part of the doorframe.

At the end of her one-year lease I gave both her and her mother a written notice that the lease would not be renewed. The day she was supposed to move I went over to discover that she had made no effort to leave. I went to several grocery stores and got 15 large boxes and brought them over to her. She promised that she would leave the next day. I couldn't see how she could move because she didn't have a car. I called her mother and asked if she was going to help her move. She said she didn't want any of that junk at her house and her daughter would have to rent a storage place to put it. She said her daughter picked up junk set out in the street for the garbage pick up and brought it home.

The second day after I brought all the boxes to her I stopped by to see the progress - None!! I asked her if she was going to rent a storage place and she said, "yes" so I drove her over to a storage rental and she paid for a month's rent. I told her I was coming back the next day with a friend who had a pick-up and we would help her pack. I also called her mother to get over there and at least take the child to her house.

The third morning my friend with the pick up arrived and we started moving her. We all packed boxes. It took 3 loads to get everything but we got her out. Thank goodness I had a large security deposit, which covered most of the repairs.

CHAPTER 15

A hard worker – A heavy drinker

Tim was a hard worker, a supervisor on the roofing job. When he was there we knew the job was being done right. He was the first man there in the morning, and the last man to leave. Some of the workers didn't like him because he wanted the job done his way – which was the right way.

He came from a good Catholic upbringing because he didn't use foul language like they often do, and he remembered holidays with a card.

Tim had one fault. He came home from work, took a shower and drank himself to sleep. Frequently, he didn't eat. He made good money, bought good things, loved classical music and listened to it by the hour on week-ends (I knew this because he rented an apartment from me and the other tenants complained about the loud music on the week-end).

He always paid his rent on time and would take time to tell me about his family – which he loved, but he was lonely. I understand that at one time he had been married but it didn't work out. His two-week's vacation was spent visiting his family in New Jersey. He'd bring back pictures of their outings and show me his mother and dad and 2 brothers.

I drove by his apartment Monday about noon and his truck was in the driveway. I thought Tim must not be well, or he'd be working. Tuesday, Wednesday, Thursday it was the same thing. I knew something was wrong. I rang the bell, no answer, so I called the police and asked for an escort to go in his apartment. The policeman arrived and I opened the door but I made him walk ahead of me because I was afraid of what we might find. The place was a disaster. There was blood on the furniture, the carpet, the bed, and the toilet was filled with blood and Kleenex. I asked the policeman to call and see if there had been a report of an accident or robbery or worse at this address. The police report said there was a 911 call on Sunday and an ambulance had taken a man to the hospital. As soon as I got the name of the hospital I rushed over there.

Tim was in a private room and looked as white as a sheet from the loss of so much blood. He said he had cirrhoses of the liver and had known it for a long time. He knew he was dying and he was crying. I asked him if he had called his family, and the nurse told me the doctor had recommended that he do so. I got the number from him and called his mother. His mother and brother flew in the next day. I also went to the main desk and asked for a priest to see him immediately. They were moving him to hospice care the next day but he passed away that night.

When I went back the next day I spoke with his mother and brother. They asked if he owed any rent – I assured them that he was paid up for the balance of the month and had a security deposit riding. His mother asked if they could come and clean up his apartment and get the security – I assured them that they could. I met them at his apartment that evening and after they walked through his mother said, "If we stayed for three months we couldn't clean this up"

Apparently he kept blacking out and falling. That was why the T.V. was turned over and a couple of chairs overturned.

Most of the furniture had to be replaced, including the mattress. The carpet was cleaned, but I replaced it anyhow. We salvaged the music equipment but that's about all.

I found pictures of the family and other papers, which I mailed to his mother. I almost felt like I had lost a member of the family I liked him so much. He had rented that apartment for five years and we had many conversations. Sometimes it seems that life just isn't fair – maybe he caused his own problem, maybe he just couldn't handle his situation.

CHAPTER 16

Jewelry Store Owners

I had a 1st floor 2 bedroom apartment for rent, and a woman called me to see the apartment. She was a nice looking lady and well dressed. She told me that she and her husband owned a jewelry store in a shopping center very close to the apartment I had for rent. She filled out an application and rented the apartment.

Everything went fine for about 10 months – and then I heard rumors that she had a big problem. Apparently her husband was involved in a "hit and run" and left the scene of the accident. The police eventually identified him and came into the jewelry store to arrest him and he pulled a gun on the officers.

I understand that he received 3 to 5 years. This left his wife in a very bad predicament. She closed the jewelry store in a couple of months and packed and moved everything that she could into the apartment. A lot of this I found out later.

About the same time her daughter was involved in an accident that wasn't her fault so she received approximately $7,000.00 in a settlement. Instead of replacing her car, she gave her mother half of the settlement and they each used the $3500.00 for a down payment on two new cars.

For a number of years the woman had attended auctions at a local jewelry auction and had made friends with the owner. I understood later that they had exchanged and purchased jewelry from each other. In order to raise rent for me she took articles from their former jewelry store and auctioned them off. She would come to my house and give me several hundred dollars at a time to put toward the rent. However, the rent was accumulating and I felt sorry for her so I didn't really pressure her for money. Also, the two car payments were not being paid so they would park the cars behind the duplex that they were renting to hide them from the dealer who was threatening to repossess them.

I got a call that the hot water tank was leaking so I went over to meet the plumber, that's when I saw how much had been moved into the apartment. There were Chinese and Japanese dolls, figurines, end tables, coffee tables, etc. There was a small walking path from the front door to the rear and a dog that she had brought home from the jewelry store where he had served as a watchdog. I didn't see or hear from her for about two weeks, but I got a call from a neighbor that the dog had been barking continuously for several days and something could be wrong.

I went to court and filed eviction papers (and that night someone picked up the dog). I was relieved for the dog because I didn't know what to do for him. I didn't want to put him in the Humane Society because I was afraid they would put him to sleep, and I didn't want to take him to a vet because I didn't know if she'd ever show up again to get him.

Somehow my friend found out where she was living. I think she filed a forwarding address at the post office, and for $1.00 you could get the forwarding address, so when I filed the eviction I had a forwarding address. By that time she owed me $1,800.00.

On the court date I appeared only to be told that the case was postponed because the daughter had called in that morning and said her mother was out of town and was unable to appear, so another date set. A week later I showed up again and an eviction was ordered.

I had to be there to point out what was mine and what was hers. As fast as the items were carried out by the sheriff's officers I had a friend put them on his truck and take them to my house where I later had a garage sale to recover some of my losses.

As soon as I put a "For Rent" sign out on the front lawn I got a call from the auctioneer that she had befriended. I saw a grown man cry. It seems that she told him she had a good client who was looking for a ring and diamond necklace so he gave her two diamond rings worth $25,000.00 each and a couple of diamond necklaces worth $20,000 on consignment to show her client. She never came back and that was a couple of weeks already. He had been by the house a number of times but didn't know where she had gone. His 100-year-old prestigious business was subsequently forced into bankruptcy.

I got a call from the daughter when she received the evection papers and she said there was a couple things that they would like to have that were family heirlooms. I told her to start talking because I had a paper and pencil ready. She read off a number of things.

The 18" T.V. some dishes, some glassware, a box of uncut stones (which did not fit the description of family heir looms) but I wrote everything down. I told her that next Sunday I leave for church at 8:00 o'clock and return 9:30 A.M. and those items would be in my garage for her to pick up and my garage would be left open.

I had a large garage sale and disposed of most of the material that had been left in the apartment. I received about $1500.00 from the garage sale, which I was grateful for. I have several items in my house, which I liked – but I still have mixed emotions toward her. None of us know how we'd react when our back is to the wall and there's no way out.

CHAPTER 17

Good Old Jimmy

Good old Jimmy was a young man about 30 years old. He and his mother came together to look at an apartment. The mother did all the looking, talking and bragging about how smart her son was. He graduated from college and met this girl who she thought was his downfall. He had been living in Chicago but had just come down to Florida to start over and live near his mother.

The mother had just remarried so she didn't think it was a good idea for him to live with them. Jimmy paid me the rent in cash but I knew who had given him the money. His mother said he was going to work with his stepfather so there would be no problem with him having the rent money in the future. He put his mother's name on the Rental Application as a reference and I saw that she lived in a beautiful home about three blocks from where I live.

Jimmy moved in and the first few months he paid his rent on time, but then Jimmy and his stepfather had a falling out so Jimmy wasn't working. I stopped by to pick up the rent when it was due and heard his hard luck story. He didn't have the rent but was looking for work and had his application in a number of places so he said he expected to have a job soon. The next few days passed and he didn't show up with any money.

I always get a lot of news through the grapevine (which in my case is from the other tenants who live in the same building). I heard that Jimmy was drunk most of the time and had no intention of looking for work. At this time his mother was not willing to pass out the money like she did when he first arrived. The chances of him coming up with the rent were slim to none.

One morning I was going to work at about 7:45 A.M. and I passed by the duplex. I saw Jimmy sitting on the front porch with a beer in his hand. I stopped, backed up and parked in front of the building. I walked up to the porch and said, "Good Morning" and then asked if he had any luck finding work. He said he wasn't looking for work any more because he was going back to Chicago. I asked him when this would happen and he said he was going to wait until the weather got warmer up there. (It was January when we were talking). I asked him how he intended to pay the rent until he left. He told me that he didn't intend to pay the rent. He had it all figured out that it would take about three months to evict him and by then it would be warmer up North and he'd have enough money to get back to Chicago. I was really burned up by his attitude and remarks.

I'm on my way to work at 7:45 A.M. He is sitting on my property telling me that he doesn't intend to pay his rent. His rent is now 3 weeks past due. I told him that I wanted him out of the apartment and off the property the next day. (This was a Friday). He laughed and shrugged his shoulders. I went to work but after work I went to the hardware store and bought two new sets of door locks keyed alike. The apartment has a knob lock on the bottom and a dead bolt lock above. I knew that if I changed the locks he couldn't get in.

He had to walk past my house to get to his mother's house, and I had seen him pass by many times on weekends. About 1:00 o'clock on Saturday afternoon I saw him come staggering down the street on his way to his mother's house. As soon as he passed by I got in my car and went to his apartment and changed the front and back door locks. I bagged up what little clothes he had and put them in a plastic garbage bag. I also put his radio and music equipment in another plastic bag and put them all in the storage shed in the backyard of the building.

I then got in my car and drove to his mother's house. I rang the bell and his mother came to the door. I asked if Jimmy was there and she said he was. I told her that he was three weeks behind in his rent and I had just evicted him. I told her that his personal belongings were in plastic bags in the storage shed behind the building and recommended that she drive over there and get them. This is a furnished apartment so the only things that he brought with him were his clothes and music equipment. I also told her that I had changed the locks on the apartment so he wouldn't be able to get back in. She seemed surprised but said she would go and get his things, and she did.

The tenant in the next-door apartment saw me changing the locks and he walked over and asked what was happening. I told him I was evicting Jimmy. He said, "I think I'll get a motel room for tonight because when he comes home and finds he's been evicted he'll really tear up things around here. I told him not to worry because I was telling him in advance before he returned. It really went very smoothly and I'm sure the most surprised person was Jimmy who intended to sit out the winter and enjoy the weather as a free loader.

I know this is not the legal way of evicting someone but sometimes it's necessary to take the bull by the horns and do what you have to do. I saved the cost of an eviction and was able to rent the apartment in a few days. I was also able to collect three month's rent that I wouldn't have gotten if he had his way. I've never heard from Jimmy or his mother again.

CHAPTER 18

What happened to Dan?

Dan was a nice looking young man – probably in his late 30's or early 40's who rented my one bedroom furnished apartment. He was driving a Van with an out of state license plate. He stayed about 3 years – but never renewed the license plate.

He told me that he had been injured in the Navy and received a monthly disability check. The injury was to his back and he did exercises on the floor of his living room every day. He said the navy hospital wanted to do surgery on his spine but he was afraid that if it didn't go right he might not be able to walk afterward. His check was automatically deposited in a bank in New York and he would call the bank when the check was due and have it transferred to a local bank (wherever he was at the time) He said he had been living overseas for three years before he came here to live.

He barely made it financially from check to check. On several occasions I had him pick up furniture with his van after I had made a purchase. Instead of paying the store to make the delivery, I would pay him the same price to pick up the merchandise. He seemed pleased to get the extra money.

In our conversations through the years he told me that he had a daughter (14 years old) and he showed me pictures of her. She lived in Colorado with her mother. He was very proud of her. Before Easter one year he made arrangements for her to come to Florida to visit him on her Spring break from school. He sent her mother the money for the plane ticket and was very excited about seeing her. Easter came and went and I didn't see the girl any place with him. I was sure he would have brought her over to my house and introduced her. When I later asked about the visit he told me that her mother decided to keep the money instead of letting her make the trip. He was very depressed over the situation and I felt bad for him because he had planned on the visit and places he would take her while she was here.

He and the man who lived next door to him were good friends and I heard one time from him that Dan had run out of money a couple days before his monthly check was due, and he was living off the grapefruit from our tree in the front yard. I took a bag of groceries over to his apartment – staples like bread, milk, peanut butter and jelly, and canned fruit. (enough for a couple days.) He was very appreciative and did little things to show his appreciation – like cleaning up the yard, washing down the front porch, etc.

I felt that I knew him pretty well from our conversations, so when he didn't pay his rent and a week passed by I went over to see what was the problem. He didn't answer the door so I knocked on his friend's door next door. He told me that he was worried about Dan because he hadn't seen him for several days. After hearing that, I used my passkey to enter the apartment.

His exercise blanket was spread out on the living room floor. There was a place setting on the table and a frozen dinner in the oven. There were clothes in the closet, a couple pair of shoes by the bed, shaving supplies in the bathroom next to the washbowl, and his personal things were still there. The pictures he showed me of his daughter were in the dresser drawer. There were 2 Afghans over a chair – ones that his mother had created. Where was Dan? His friend next door and I called the police and reported him as a missing person. We called all the local hospitals but they had no record of him being there. His van was still in front of the house. Where was he??????

I waited another two weeks before I started boxing up his clothes and belongings. I took them to my home and kept them in the garage for at least a year. He never showed up and I never heard from him again. This bothered me terribly. In my mind I went through every possible scenario. Was he kidnapped??? Did he have a loss of memory and was he wandering around lost?? Why didn't he say "Good Bye" to his friend next door?? Did he meet with foul play when he picked up his check??? I'll never know but I'll still hope that some day, some time, I'll get a phone call from him explaining what happened.

We never found the title to the Van, which he left parked out in front of the apartment. When I talked to his friend who lived next door I was told that Dan didn't have the title and that's why he didn't update the license every year. It still had the same license plate on that was there when he arrived. Another mystery.

Chapter 19

A Friend wants In

My doorbell rang and when I answered the door a young man was standing there. I knew he was a friend of one of my tenants because I had seen my tenant standing in front of his apartment talking to him in his car.

He told me he had to get in John's apartment because he left something inside from the night before and he needed it and John wasn't home.

I explained that I couldn't let him in and he would have to wait until John got home to get in. He became very aggravated and told me he was going to get in whether I unlocked the door for him or not. In fact, he said he'd kick the door in if he had to. The door was a glass jalousie door with a protective grill on the inside protecting the glass and also making sure the glass couldn't be broken to gain entrance.

I closed the door and went to the phone and dialed the police department. I explained the situation to the operator and he said she'd have someone over to the apartment. I got in my car and drove over there, but he had already accomplished what he set out to do.

Apparently he was wearing heavy boots because he kicked right through the glass and tore the grill away from one side so he could reach in and unlock the door and get in.

My tenant was on disability and his sister was appointed guardian so I had her phone number and I called her. The police arrived close behind me and proceeded to make out a police report.

About then my tenant and his sister drove up to the building and the police were talking to them. He told them that his friend had left some drugs at the house from a party the night before because he noticed that they were there when he left.

The police drove my tenant over to his friend's house. Of course, his friend wasn't home but his mother immediately got in her car and drove over to the apartment. I was still there and she apologized for her son and begged me not to press charges because she would pay for a new door and for having it painted.

Personally, I think it was wrong for her to cover up for him. He should have been made to face the consequences of his behavior. However, it was the easy way out for me to resolve the problem.

The next morning she called me and told me she had called the door company and she gave me the name and phone number to verify the information. They came out the next day measured up the door and installed a new solid-wood door. Then she paid my tenant $50.00 to prime coat and paint the door. I didn't think he should have been rewarded either. But it all worked out to my benefit.

CHAPTER 20

A Volunteer Painter

I rented the one bedroom duplex to a young couple that arrived driving a large SUV. They were both employed. She was a waitress at a local restaurant and he was a cook at a different restaurant.

After a few months he decided to change the color of the walls in the living room without discussing it with me. The lease states that the tenant will not make major repairs or paint walls without the landlord's permission. He purchased a gallon of pink paint I discovered later, and was going to paint the living room walls. I only use one color on the walls of all my apartments. It is an off white color which goes with everything and is accepted by everyone regardless of what their favorite color is. I always have a gallon of paint on hand so if I need to touch up or paint only one wall, it will match the rest of the room.

He brought the paint home and set it down in the living room on the carpet in front of the couch. Apparently when he sat down on the couch he kicked the open bucket of paint and it splashed on the carpet. The pink paint covered an area of approximately 15" x 15". Not knowing what to do, he cut that area out of the carpet. The carpet was less than a year old and there were several extra pieces of carpet left over so we put them in front of the outside doors to use as doormats. He cut a piece out of the extra carpet and tried to fit it in the area he had cut out. It was a very sloppy fit so he put a throw rug over it and set the coffee table on the throw rug.

After a year they decided to go back up North so they told me they were leaving. They asked me if I would refund the security deposit when they left because they were short of money and needed it for their trip back home. When they were ready to leave I went to the apartment and did a "walk through". Everything looked neat and clean so I gave them the security money they had paid when they moved in. I know better than to do this but sometime my heart makes decisions instead of my head.

The next day I went to the apartment to put the final touch on the clean up and to wash the bed linens and towels. When I moved the throw rug under the coffee table to run the vacuum I discovered the piece of carpet that had been cut out. The living room carpet was too new to have it replaced so I purchased a 5 x 8 area rug and put it over the cut out carpet. I showed the new tenant the cut out under the coffee table so he would know that I wouldn't hold him responsible for it.

CHAPTER 21

Renting To Relatives

Renting to relatives is very touchy. In the first place they feel that they have special privileges because they are in the family. They don't feel that they have to sign a lease, or put up a security Deposit. A single male relative came down to Florida and stayed with my Sister and her husband while he looked around to find a place to rent. Fortunately (or unfortunately) a vacancy came up in one of my apartments. He visited the apartment and decided it was just what he was looking for. He assured me that he would stay for a long period of time – probably for years (Famous last words). Without discussing it with me, he painted the kitchen a royal blue color.

After a few months he found a girl friend and spent 3 or 4 nights a week at her place. Then his son and his son's girlfriend decided to come down to Florida, so without discussing it with me, he moved in with his girlfriend and allowed his son and his girlfriend to move in his apartment. After a couple months they decided to go back north, and my original tenant decided to stay permanently at his girlfriend's house, so I had a vacant apartment.

Millie

When I went over to check the apartment to rent –
I discovered a large crack in the shower door. It was too
dangerous to leave so I replaced the shower doors. When I
discussed this with my relative, he insisted it was not there
when he moved, so he would write to His son and send him
a copy of the bill. Of course, His son knew nothing about
it. When this developed into a family problem, I paid for
the doors myself, painted the kitchen a nice "Antique white"
Color, and absorbed the cost.

CHAPTER 22

A Sad Story For Mother And Son

A mother and son came to see an apartment I had for rent. They seemed pleased with the apartment and decided to rent it. The mother explained that her son had been sick for a period of time but was now on the road to recovery. She said she would pay the rent for a few months until he was well and got a job.

She kept her word and sent a check for the next three months but the fourth month I did not receive a check so I called her to discuss the situation.

I was told that things had not worked out and her son would be taking over the rent payments. I went to the apartment to make sure he knew he would be responsible for the rent in the future. He got out of bed to answer the door. He said he was spending most of his time in bed.

He told me that he was HIV positive and his mother had reached the "end of the line" and could not afford to pay his rent. However, he was not getting better and was applying to Social Services for help. He said he turned in my name, as "Landlord" and I would be hearing from them. After about ten days I received a letter and check for the rent. This continued for about three months and then I did not receive a check.

When I went to the apartment to see what was happening I was told that the Social Service Agency had found a place for him to live but it would not be available until the 1st of the next month. I asked him what he expected me to do for the present month's rent.

He told me that if he could, he would gladly get out voluntarily so I wouldn't have to start eviction proceedings. He didn't want to cause me any trouble. However, he had no place to go. He said he would have to sit on the porch or the curb until Social Services was ready to come for him. I agreed to let him stay until they had a place for him. They came and picked him up the 1st of the next month.

I bought rubber gloves and disinfectant and proceeded to clean the apartment. I replaced the bed linens, towels and blankets. My heart ached for this young man and his family. However, I felt that I had been drawn into a situation that I was not aware of. They had not been honest with me from day one - or perhaps his mother didn't know that he had " Aids". Maybe she believed that he was going to get better and get a job when he moved in. What heartache!

CHAPTER 23

Too Many People For A Small Room

A young man in his mid 20's called to see an efficiency apartment I had for rent. He decided to rent the apartment and paid the 1st month's rent and the Security deposit.

He told me he came from Massachusetts and had the promise of a job in a local restaurant. He had his clothes with him so he moved in at once. The building is located a couple blocks from a bus station, so I presumed that he had come to Florida by bus. I left the building – but in about a week I got a call from one of the other tenants inquiring as to how many people rented the efficiency. They said there were a lot of people coming and going in that apartment. I promised to come by and investigate.

The next morning I went to the apartment and rapped on the door. A man answered the door – not the one I rented to, and when I asked him who he was I was told that he was a friend. I heard a conversation in the background so I asked where my tenant was. I was told that he was at work. I asked when he would be home and was told he would be there around 5 P.M. I left and returned about 5:30 P.M.

I found my tenant at home and asked how many people were staying in the efficiency. I was told that four of his friends from Massachusetts were staying with him. They had come to Florida to work during the Tourist Season.

I referred him back to the lease he had signed that stated that there would be one person living in the apartment. He said he had been staying with them in Massachusetts during the summer and didn't see why they couldn't all bunk up together for the winter.

I told him that I would file for an eviction unless they moved out. However, I told him I would refund the entire amount of money he had given me if they would find another place immediately. Apparently that offer was acceptable, because he said they would leave within a week and they did.

Having a vacant apartment again means I have to wash bed linens, towels, and in most cases - dirty dishes, but it's a lot cheaper than going for an eviction. There's no way five grown men could live in a one room efficiency for four or five months.

CHAPTER 24

The Odd Couple

When they came to look at the apartment they could have told me they were mother and son, and I would have accepted that. However, they were truly husband and wife. He appeared to be in his middle 30's and she was probably in her late 50's or early 60's. There was at least 25 years difference in their age.

He was about 6 ft. tall and she was about 5'2" and on the heavy side. She did all the talking and told me they had just come to Florida from a small town in Illinois. She worked in a beauty shop and he had just come home from the army when they met. Later when we were talking, she told me that he told her all he wanted from his marriage was a wife willing to give him sex when he wanted it, and to cook his meals for him when he came home from work. I guess this is what they agreed on because they were married.

They joined a nudist camp here in Florida and spent their weekends there. They did not wear any clothes when they were alone at home either. When I came to pick up the rent check there was always a wait at the door while they put on some clothes. I knew this was how they lived so I was prepared to wait

They lived in the apartment for 5 years when they decided to go to Illinois to visit her son. They told me they would be gone for about a month, and paid their rent in advance. They were driving their car but only got as far as South Carolina, when they had an automobile accident. A trailer truck pulled out of a truck stop and hit their car broadside. The car was totaled and he was in the hospital for about a week. When they finally got back home he didn't go to work for several months, and then he was back in the hospital again. I went to see him in the hospital one evening where he told me the doctor told him he would not be able to go back to work because his job required him to be on his feet a lot. His leg and foot were severely injured in the accident.

They hired a lawyer to try to get a settlement for the accident, but it was a complicated case. They were residents of Florida, the accident happened in South Carolina, and the owner of the truck that hit them had a business in Pennsylvania. They changed lawyers several times but couldn't find one who was interested enough to really pursue the case and spend the time and money it required. They didn't have any money so the lawyers weren't interested.

They had no income and were using up their savings so they decided to go back to Illinois and live with her son. I felt very sorry for them because their future did not look good.

CHAPTER 25

A Son On Drugs

One night about 10 O'clock my doorbell rang. I peeked thru the window to see who was there. Standing in front of my door was a lady who I recognized as a tenant in the one bedroom duplex I owned. I opened the door and when she came in I saw that she had been crying. She was probably 40 to 45 years old and had lived in the apartment for 5 years without any problems.

I put my arms around her and asked what had happened to make her cry. She told me that her son had come to her apartment that night, high on drugs and asking to borrow money. When she refused to give him any money he hit her and knocked her against the wall. She ordered him to leave but he refused to leave. She ran out the back door and drove to my house. She said, "You're the landlord, so I want you to come down to my apartment and tell him to leave." I told her "You're his mother and he knocked you against the wall, so he isn't going to respect me. He'll probably knock me against the wall too."

She told me he was on probation for selling drugs and had been in jail. He had a court date for the next morning and he was probably having a last drug party before going back to jail.

I knew she was a secretary at a doctor's office so I asked her if she could go to work the next morning in the clothes she was wearing. She said she could, so the best solution to her problem was for her to spend the night in my spare bedroom. She felt that he would be gone the next day. She spent the night at my house and went to work the next morning. At the end of the day when she went home he was gone. A few months later, she moved to a condominium a couple blocks away. She rented a condo apartment on the 4th floor. She said she felt safer on the 4th floor because in her building there is security at the front entrance. Also, the only entrance to her apartment is higher than ground level. She lives alone and I can understand her need for added security.

CHAPTER 26

Three Vietnamese Refugees

At the end of the Vietnam War our government worked with churches to find homes for refugees. Our church signed a contract with the government that included housing a few for one year and finding them employment. I had a one-bedroom apartment vacant so I volunteered it for our church to house whoever we drew as refugees. We were assigned three young men. Several members of our church donated money for the rent, and a committee was set up to help them get established. When they arrived, the language difference was a challenge. Several members met them at the airport and drove them to their apartment. When they walked in their apartment one inquired, "Is this where you live?" We were pleased to tell them that it was where they were going to live.

The oldest of the group was approximately 24 years old. He spoke understandable English, so he was the spokesman for the other two. We stocked the refrigerator with what we considered to be staple food, but soon found out that their diets were a lot different from ours, so we ended up taking them with us grocery shopping where they could pick out their choice of food.

We found jobs for each of them, and had church members ride the bus to and from work with each one of them until they recognized the bus they needed to get back and forth from home to work. They pooled their money and after about a year the oldest one told me they wanted to look at used cars.

I took them around to look at cars and did all the negotiating for them. They found a Honda that they could afford so they made the purchase. Then I took them for insurance and a driver's license. The oldest one took an oral test and got a license, so they were very happy to be independent and able to go shopping by themselves. They managed to keep track of other refugees who came over at the same time they did and they visited back and forth.

The two oldest told me that they had worked at an American army base in Vietnam and when the word came to evacuate, the Americans who were leaving helped them get on planes to get over here. They felt that if they had stayed in Vietnam they would have been considered traitors by the North Vietnamese and would have been severely punished. I was told that the oldest of the three had left behind a wife and baby. He grieved over this and wondered if they would ever be reunited.

Years have passed since our paths crossed. I think about them often and now that travel is open between our countries I hope they have been able to reunite with their families.

CHAPTER 27

It's Later Than We Think

I rented an apartment to a retired couple that was building a home here in Florida so they wanted to be in the area while the house was under construction. They signed a one-year lease because they were sure it would be a year before their house would be completed. They said they had been planning for many years to move to Florida for their "Golden Years" and had visited the area many times on their vacations.

They sold their home in New Jersey where they both had lived and worked. They had three children and their children were looking forward to spending their vacations here in Florida visiting their parents. They were going to have a swimming pool in their new home for their kids and grandchildren to enjoy. Their furniture was shipped down from New Jersey and was put in storage while the new house was under construction. They were so happy and talked constantly about how great it was going to be to leave the cold winters back in New Jersey and sit here and soak up the sun.

About two months after they moved in they went out to dinner at a local restaurant. The husband got a piece of meat caught in his throat and he choked to death before help arrived to save him.

Their children came down, not for a joyful vacation, but to make arrangements for their father's funeral and to take their mother back with them. They had to ship the furniture back to New Jersey and make arrangements with the builder to withdraw from the contract to build the new house. What a sad ending to their hopes and dreams. It's a lesson to each one of us to enjoy every day because we have no guarantee that there will be a tomorrow.

CHAPTER 28

Do Your Homework
Before You Move

Many people from the north dream of retiring in Florida when they retire. I was one of them, but I didn't wait to retire to come to Florida. Before making that decision, there are a number of things you must do.

First, I would suggest that you come to Florida and spend some time on the West coast of Florida and then come to the East Coast for a time. I know many people who live on the West Coast in Tampa, Sarasota, or Naples who wouldn't think of living on the East coast, and then there are some who think just the opposite. Even after you decide on which side of Florida suits you best there are areas of each city to check out.

A friend in Michigan decided to sell her home and come to Florida and buy a condominium. Everyone is not adapted to condominium living after living in a house.

She rented out her home in Michigan for a year and came down to Florida and rented a two-bedroom condominium for a year to see how well she liked living in a condo. This also gave her time to check out the area to see if she was comfortable in this location. I'm happy to say that she loved living in the condo.

There were some disadvantages such as using a community laundry room when she was used to having a laundry room in her own home. Another disadvantage was having an assigned parking spot, when she was used to having a garage attached to her house.

However, there were many advantages that she enjoyed such as no lawn maintenance, no roof problems, and no outside painting or other home maintenance costs. She enjoyed the fact that she could lock the front door and go on vacation without worrying about her apartment. After a year she decided to sell her home up North and buy an apartment in the building where she had been renting. She liked the location and the people who lived in the building. The condominium she bought had a swimming pool that her children and grandchildren could enjoy and she didn't have to worry about pool maintenance. Some condos have weekly social events such as card games, movies, cook outs, pot- lucks, bingo games, parties on all the holidays, and many more. This helps to make new friends and keep from getting lonesome.

I had another friend who came down to live and was so lonesome for her former friends and family that she went back up North to her old neighborhood to live again. Retiring at a new location is a big decision and doing your homework before making the change will save money and make life a lot more pleasant.

CHAPTER 29

Exchanged Furniture

A tenant moved out so I went to the apartment to fix it up for the next tenant. This means washing the dishes, silverware, bed linens and towels, running the vacuum and replacing whatever furniture needs replacing because all my apartments are furnished. This time I replaced the couch and the kitchen table and 4 chairs. I bought them at a local consignment store. They delivered the furniture and I was very satisfied that the apartment looked good.

Sometimes when I have a vacant apartment, I leave the back door unlocked. I put my "For Rent" sign in the front yard with my phone number on it, and tell the tenant in the apartment next door that the door is unlocked and the apartment is vacant. That's so that if they see someone walking thru they know it's with my permission. I have often remarked, "If you see a moving van loading up my furniture, call me". Of course, I don't expect this to happen.

The reason I leave the door unlocked is that it saves a lot of unnecessary trips back and forth. When I get a phone call from someone parked in front of the building with a cell phone, who wants to see the apartment, I can tell them

"The back door is open". I tell them to walk through and if they're interested in renting the apartment to call me and I'll meet them there.

I received a call from a man who had walked thru, liked what he saw, and wanted to meet me to rent the apartment. I went to the apartment and was really surprised at what I saw. There was a different couch in the living room, not the one I had just purchased, and a different table and chairs in the kitchen. I recognized them as coming from the apartment next door. I never said anything to the man I was there to meet because he already told me on the phone that he liked the apartment. After he signed a lease and gave me a check I gave him the keys and went to the apartment next door. I was very upset and asked them what right they had to move furniture from one apartment to the other without my permission and this had better not ever happen again. At this point there wasn't anything to do except to express my anger. They didn't think that they had done anything that bad and apologized. After all, they said they didn't steal anything. They thought the couch matched their other furniture better than the one they had, and they liked the kitchen furniture so they just exchanged them.

I find that after this many years in the rental business there's always another surprise around the corner.

CHAPTER 30

The Trespasser

I received a phone call from a young man who was interested in renting my one bedroom apartment. He met me at the apartment liked it and said he would like to bring his uncle over later when he got off work. They were both living separately and decided to get an apartment together to save money.

About 7:00 P.M. I received another call stating that he and his uncle would like to meet me at the apartment. We met and they decided to rent it. It was a furnished apartment and consisted of a living room, kitchen, bedroom, bath and a glassed in porch. A door from the bedroom opened to the porch. The porch had an outside door, which opened to the back yard. There was a double bed in the bedroom and I called the consignment shop and had them deliver twin beds and pick up the double bed.

The uncle signed a one-year lease and gave me the rent and security. I went to K Mart and bought new bedding for twin beds and they moved in the next weekend.

I understood later that the nephew moved one twin bed, a dresser, one of the nightstands and a lamp out to the porch making himself a separate bedroom.

About 3 months went by when I got a call from the tenant at the other end of the building. He said they had a party the night before and he was up all night from the noise. I told him to call me while the party was in progress if it ever happened again and I also stopped in the evening and discussed this with the uncle and his nephew. It seems the uncle was out of town for the weekend but they assured me that it would never happen again.

About a month later I got a phone call at 2:00 A.M. from the tenant who had complained before. He said he was following my instructions and informing me that a party was in full bloom. I got dressed and drove over there. Both the front door and the back door were wide open and every light in the apartment was on. There were about 8 people in the apartment with a cigarette in one hand and a drink in the other.

There were three or four cars parked in front on the lawn. I walked in the front door and stood there. Someone turned down the music and I asked "What's going on?" Three or four scooted out the front door and the nephew left by the back door. I said "The party's over and I want every one out" I turned out the lights and closed and locked the doors and left.

The next evening I was down there and the uncle was very surprised that it had happened again when he was gone. He told me that he was putting his nephew out.

I had serious sickness in my family at this time and was spending most of the day and part of the evening visiting at the hospital. I did not want to get involved in this problem at this time because I thought the uncle could take care of it.

I got a call from the tenant in the apartment at the other end of the building. He was self-employed and drove a pick-up truck He parked his truck in the back of the apartment where we had two parking spaces. He usually had small supplies and a few tools in the truck but nothing had ever been missing. He said there were a lot of people coming past his door going to the porch. Some of his tools were missing from the truck and he was suspicious of the strangers coming and going through the yard. Although he had no proof as to who took the tools he said he did not feel safe leaving anything in the truck anymore.

The next time the uncle came to pay his rent I asked him if the situation between him and his nephew had been resolved. To my surprise he told me that the situation had gotten worse.

His nephew wasn't working and was not contributing to the cost of food or the rent. He would go out and not come home until 2:00 A.M. or later. When he came home he headed for the kitchen, checked the refrigerator and made himself something to eat. He said the lights were all turned on and the odor of food cooking usually woke him up. This was upsetting because he had to go to work in the morning.

They got into violent arguments and several times the police were called. The uncle now changed the locks on the front door and locked the passage door from the bedroom to the porch. This meant that the nephew had no use of the bathroom. He in turn changed the lock on the porch so his uncle could not get in

I felt that I now had to get involved so I made out a Three Day Notice to vacate the property and went and talked to the nephew. I told him I did not want him living on the porch. He said he'd look around and try to find a place to move to. I told him I'd be back in three days and I hope he was gone.

I went back in three days and of course, he was still there. He told me that this was his legal residence and he intended to stay. I left and went home and called my lawyer and asked his advice. He told me that he would take the case but it would cost $800.00 to go to court for an eviction. I told him to forget it.

I then called the police station and asked them if there was any way they could help me. To my surprise the lady officer told me that our city has a No Trespassing law and I would probably qualify under the terms of that law. She told me to come to the station and pick up the paper work to register as a property owner.

I picked up the paper work and application to register. It required a notarized signature so I filled out the paper and went directly to the bank to a notary. I then drove back to the police station and filed the registration.

There were two pages of instructions and I noticed that one of the lines said "If you qualify" so I waited 3 days and called the station to make sure I qualified. The officer said I did and asked if I had a problem. I told her my problem and she said a police officer would meet me at the duplex in 15 minutes.

We both pulled up in front of the building at the same time from different directions. I got out with my paper work and explained the situation to the officer. We both walked around the building to the porch door. She told me to stand back while she talked to the nephew.

She was very polite but very stern. She rapped on the door and the nephew answered. She asked him to identify himself by name and told him that I had made a complaint that he was trespassing and I wanted him to leave. He told her "this is my legal residence". She asked him if he was paying rent to anyone. He answered, "No". She then told him that he was trespassing and he had until 4:00 P.M. to vacate the property. She asked him if he understood and he replied "Yes" She said, "If I come back at 4:30 P.M. and you are still here you will be arrested and go to Jail. Do you understand?" He answered "Yes" and we both left.

I drove by about 3:30 P.M. to see if there .was any action going on and there was a car backed up to his door and he and another man were carrying out white plastic bags so I knew he was leaving.

I came back at 5:00 P.M. and he and his belongings were gone.

It was a matter of getting the right person to help. I guess that applies to a lot of situations.

CHAPTER 31

Who Owns The Vehicle?

I was sitting in my comfortable tilt-back-chair watching T.V. when my phone rang about 6:30 P.M.

I answered the phone to hear one of my tenants's telling me that she was in an accident. She said that she was at the scene of the accident that she was involved in. The police and an ambulance were there also. She said she was driving Jeff's car (Jeff is one of my other tenants who lives next door to her)

She said she needed to contact Jeff because she couldn't find the registration or insurance papers in the glove compartment of the car and the police were waiting for her to produce these papers.

She asked me to contact Jeff on his cell phone and give him her cell phone number to call immediately. She did not have his cell phone number with her. I asked her if she was hurt and she replied, "Yes".

I told her I'd call him immediately and hung up.

I called and he answered. I told him that Kathy was in a car accident with his car and needed him to call her immediately at the number I would give him. He said he was driving in traffic and asked me to hold the line until he was able to pull to the side of the road and find a paper and pencil. I held the line and gave him the number Kathy had given me.

I waited until about 8:30 P.M. and then called Kathy's cell phone number. Jeff answered.

I asked how she was and he said he was at the hospital where they were doing tests to see about her injuries. He said she was behind a bus that had stopped when another car crashed into the back of her car pushing her partially under the back of the bus. The car she was driving was completely destroyed beyond repair.

This was bad enough except that there's more to the story. Jeff's son who was 26 years old died last January from a drug overdose. He worked with his father and his father had taken it very hard. The car that Kathy was driving belonged to Jeff's son. Jeff said it has just been sitting idle since January because he couldn't bring himself around to selling it. It was sitting at the apartment with a "For Sale" sign on it, which is where Kathy saw it.

The reason Kathy was driving Jeff's car was because her car was parked in front of the apartment in our circle drive when she heard a loud crash about 3:00 A.M. the night before. Someone was driving too fast when they reached the corner and couldn't make the curve around the Turnaround, which is in the center of the two streets, which come together and they came up on the front lawn and hit her car.

She got dressed and went outside but the other car was gone. The next morning she took her car to the repair shop but it wouldn't be ready for 3 days. She saw the "For Sale" sign on Jeff's car so she talked to Jeff and told him she would like to buy his car and sell hers when she got it back. In fact she took his car to her repair shop and had the mechanic check it over and make a few minor repairs at a cost of $400.00.

They now have a big problem. Who owns the car?

Jeff had not registered the car in his name after his son's death. It was still in his son's name. The insurance had expired and Jeff did not renew it so Kathy was driving a car without insurance for which she got a $100.00 ticket.

Who owns the car? And who should the insurance company be dealing with.

Kathy's injuries consisted of a fractured shoulder and arm and whip lash to her neck (plus bruises to her chest and legs). I understand that she has a lawyer to represent her and I see her driving her original car. I imagine this will be a long drawn out case before it is settled.

Chapter 32

In Conclusion

I highly recommend income property as an Investment for retirement.

I have owned and managed 4 pieces of income Property and I believe that has kept me active.

I believe it is important to recognize that this is a business and not get too upset when things go wrong. Just as in any other business, there are ups and downs.

It is important to have a good plumber who you can depend on when you need him. It seems that every plumbing problem comes to a head on the weekend. This has happened so many times that I can't begin to count them.

I was very lucky to have a son and two grandsons who were always willing to help when needed.

I always had lawn service although most of the tenants volunteered to "cut the grass" when they first moved in. I never asked a tenant to do any work around the building. It's always best to hire outside help-someone who is licensed and insured

I have only had to go to court twice for an eviction. The first step to evict a tenant is to give them a "3 Day Notice to

Pay Rent or Deliver Possession" It's a standard form available at Office Depot. That usually brings the situation to a head. They either leave or make arrangements to come up with the rent. If they don't, the next step is to file for a Court Hearing and that costs between $250.00 and $350.00.

At that filing the court is supplied with a copy of the lease and a copy of the 3 Day Notice which shows how much back rent is due.

After that the sheriff delivers a copy of these papers to the tenant and they have 10 days to file an answer. After the 10 days both tenant and landlord receive a letter with a court date and time for the hearing. Only twice have I had to go that far to evict a tenant. It's expensive and time consuming and it's always better to stay out of court .

I'm 89 yrs. old now and I only own one duplex and my home. That's enough to keep me busy.

Author's Biography

Mildred Grady, the author, was born in Detroit Michigan in 1920. She and her husband were self-employed and when they retired, they didn't have a pension. They bought income property in Florida in 1961, 1962 and at one time owned 4 properties with a total of 12 rental units.

Mr. Grady died in 1982 so she managed the property with the help of her son and two grandsons. Now at the age of 89, she owns one triplex and manages the property herself.